Of Earth

& Fire

Artwork & Poems

Vijali Hamilton

WORLD WHEEL PRESS
vijali@worldwheelpress.org
www.worldwheelpress.org

ISBN-13: 978-0-9789055-0-7
ISBN-10: 0-9789-0550-4
Library of Congress Control Number: 2006937046
Printed in the United States of America
This book is printed on acid-free paper.

Cover art by Vijali Hamilton
Cover design by Henry Swan III and Sara Glaser
Book design by Vijali Hamilton and Karen Fisher
Design consulting and image editing by Henry Swan III

Order copies from
WORLD WHEEL PRESS
www.worldwheelpress.org

Prologue

I lived in retreat for five years, alone at the top of a mountain. In a dream I was asked to reenter the world, circling the globe building community through the creation of monumental stone sculptures and performance ceremonies. It was a pilgrimage that took me seven years, living and working in twelve countries around the world. If there is any wisdom running through my life now, in my walking on this earth, it has come from listening in the Great Silence to the stones, the trees, and the open spaces, to the wild animals, to the pulse of all life as my own heartbeat. I offer these poems and the artwork that have emerged, as a prayer for peace.

Vijali

Dedicated
to Our Earth Family

EARTH ~ *Blood Red*

WATER ~ *Rivers Of Heart*

FIRE ~ *Fire Under Stone*

AIR ~ A Dry Leaf Falls

ETHER ~ Soluble

EARTH

Blood Red

Plate 1

Blood Red

Blood red earth,
rising plateaus,
folds of this valley—
these are the body
of my mother—
they hold me.
The red aura of anger
seen around me
by an Indian sage
has been dissolved
in earth
tingeing the sunsets
cast on mesa walls.

This red land is me,
my history
written in stone.

Castle Valley, Utah
September 2003

The Earth in Love

She lifted her head as the sun rose
    and her earth body flowed
        like the rivers before her.
Out of the earth's heart
    red molten stone
        baked the clay of her thighs.
For the first time earth walked.
For the first time she talked
through red lips, finding words,
    echo of mountains
        rush of streams
            wind through canyons.

The earth gave a sigh
as shadows crept over her arms.
Her song filled the
    oncoming darkness
        with dreams
            of the earth
                in love.

Malibu, California
July 1999

Plate 2

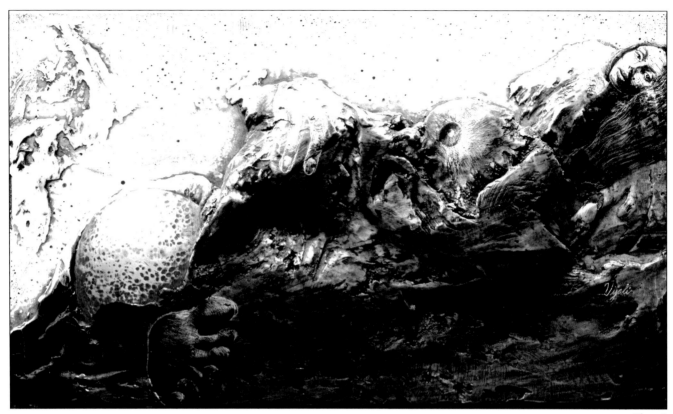

Plate 3

Fierce Love of the Wild

I walked the red earth at sunrise
down a path among witnessing stones
that stood in attention for centuries
to wind and snow, to each passer-by.
A shadow caught my eye
and I crawled into a cave laced with cobwebs,
dirt pawed to a fine dust,
soft and silky for a bed.

I groped through layers of the past
uncovered an Anasazi scraper.
Returning the flaked stone to its ledge,

not disturbing its ancient home,
I wondered where the fierce love
of the wild is buried today.

Often I cry into dark jaws of earth
and kiss the warm mouth of winds—
looking for that wildness
where my soul can root.

Castle Valley, Utah
May 1996

Alone

Alone,
Locked in a dog kennel,
my pink body smeared
with dried excrement,
tears streak my cheeks,
my eyes are glazed with fear.
I am hungry and eat the shit
on my hands and feet,
I am thirsty and want my mommy—
I am two years old.

Foster homes,
bruises on my face—
I am sent to Grandma's house.
Through the front door
I watch the children walk
down our tree-lined street
holding the hands of parents—
forehead pressed against the screen,
"Why am I the only child
 without a mommy and daddy?"
 Grandma does not answer.

Castle Valley, Utah
May 2005

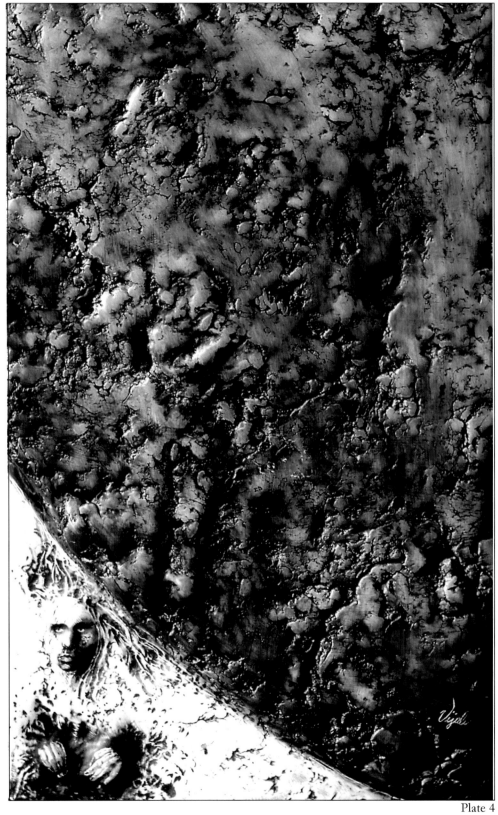

Plate 4

Plate 5

Frozen Dreams

I turn to Grandma,
"What happened
to my mommy?"
Grandma says,
"She thinks she is
the Virgin Mary,
that is why she's
locked away."
    "Paranoid
    schizophrenic,"
    doctors say.
    "Brain damaged
    from shock treatment
    early in her stay,"
    her records say.
    "Two times
    she ran away.
    But now
    the treatment
    is successful;
    she is quiet, helpful,
    does not run away,"
    her papers say.
    "Now, you can see her,
    doctors say,
    "catatonic two years,
    she's coming 'round."
I am sixteen
and waiting
in the lounge
with butterflies
in my stomach
remembering
Mommy
graceful and
so beautiful.

Then she opens
the door, sits down,
does not move,
but looks at me
not saying words,
a stare not seeing,
teeth pulled out,
bloated flesh,
hair growing from
her swollen face.
    Frozen dreams
    on thorazine
    carry Mamma
    to her death.
The relatives say,
"Oh, what relief
she passed away."
    And now her breath
    freed from fear
    and medication
    runs through my art.
    My feet are walking
    her unborn dreams.

Castle Valley, Utah
September 1996

Plate 6

Black Box

Lift me from this box
I pray
and give me wisdom.
Lift me from this darkness
I ask
and give me sight.

Santa Barbara, California
1972

Plate 7

Voiceless

In her pink pinafore,
she slipped out back
and softly closed the door.
So shy, she was so very shy
and often talked with shapes
she recognized in clouds;
Jesus, eagle, dolphin, whale.
Skipping down the street
she played hop-scotch
until she stood before
the corner candy store.

She pressed her face
against the window pane.
Colored sweets
were in bright jars
wrapped in shining foil,
red, and blue, and pink.

You offered her a candy
if she would come behind the door.
You lifted her upon your knee,
her blue eyes questioning.
You slid your dancing fingers
under her pink pinafore
and reaching for her sweet place,
began to open pain in her.

Before that day,
she did not know the smell of semen;
the sticky corridors of desire—
a wound she would carry silently.

Grandma asked, "You must tell me,
Honey, what is on your mind."
She was so tiny, she stood upon a stool.
The Judge leaned over, said to her,
"Speak louder, we cannot hear."
But no sound rose from her pursed lips
as she stared at her father, grandma,
strangers, and *you* sitting there.

Castle Valley, Utah
September 5, 1996

Depression
Fear
and anger.

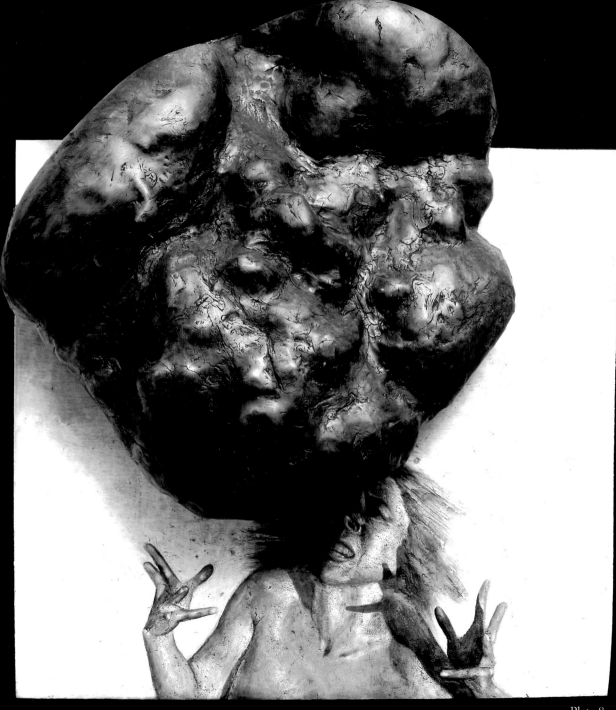

Plate 8

Unraveling

Unraveling
marriage. A wife—
free maid, accountant,
cook and dishwasher,
raising step-children,
bread winner too—
where does it end,
as the spirit shrinks
and longs for space
to thrive.

A jumble of dishes, laundry on washer,
pants sprawled on the floor where he left them.
I do not rush to straighten the house
but lay my hand on his shoulder,
sit on the arm of his chair—he clicks off TV.
Can he feel my love in the pain of this silence?
Tears stream down my lips, my throat.
Beneath my hand, I feel the pulse of fear
in a man I love. His eyes close
as if the pressure of truth is too much.
His head droops and the chair
grows in size holding him in sleep.

I stand, still with my hand on his sleeping form,
and look out the window. I see fog rolling in,
covering the coast, luminous.
The thunder in my gut subsides.
Light from the window
falls on me, fills me.
Then in sleep,
he pulls away,
and silently I
leave a decade
of life
I had known.

Castle Valley, Utah
June 2005

Plate 9

Through the Portal

Two boulders form the portal:

one gray granite stone stands tall, piercing sky
his flame-shaped presence fierce and stately,
orange, black, and yellow lichen are his skin,
etched spiral in his flesh where one plant thrives.

The other stone, female, planted in dark earth,
her rounded granite shoulders supporting sky,
her hollowed belly shaping space,
she welcomes all to find a place of rest.

Three claps of thunder from a cloudless sky
and through the portal stones we run across the green,
sunflowers attend, a burst of spring, and pears in trees,
the shape of woman, fall to the ground

as magnificent frigate birds sing. Like children
we gather stones and shape them in a ring:
bird stone, bear stone, butterfly, whale and snake—
in this family circle laughing we all know our place.

La, la, la!   La, la li!   La, li, la, la!   La, la, li!   La, li, la li!

Christina Lake, Canada
June 1999

Plate 10

Family of Earth

She gathered fragments of her self:
divorced woman, unknown artist, poet,
shy girl, passionate woman, wise crone,
and walked out of town into the hills.

Silence swept over her, a medicine
for wounds as she walked
on the earth path leading nowhere.
What a relief not to hold the hand of desire!

Freedom entered her stride, her taut legs
spread with each step and drew into her body
cool night air. She walked in silence. Stillness
followed her, surrounded her, entered her.

As she mounted the rock at top of the knoll
she felt the dark root of her breath, before lava,
before rain, before sun, before the beginning of time.
The air was crisp, the rock warm, the sky red.

She could see the town in the distance, could feel
the pulling of lives along its long roads. She could hear
fathers and mothers coming home from work.
Dogs barking, children playing, the screech of car wheels.

All the while, she stood on warm granite,
rooted to earth, searching plant and animal kin
through sage-tinged breeze. Town faded
into darkness, and she knew her place.

Castle Valley, Utah
March 1999

Animal Am I

Ancient stories
tell of human beings taking animal bodies,
looking through eyes of mountain lion,
calling through cry of bird.
I feel myself as animal
trapped in the gangly human stride,
hairless, unadorned.
I am home when roaming solitary
  among the bush and stone,
    awake to stars and blackness of night.
      Tongue-tied with words,
        I howl and hoot.
          Silence descends.
            My fingertips speak only
              the language of skin.
Pungent smell of sage
and taste of sweat inspire.
But chatter is empty,
a rattling of sound in space.
My eyes are alert for a gesture of hand,
curve of a spine,
fullness of breath,
loosening bones,
softening flesh.
            Animal I am
            sunning on stone
            with my lizard friend.

West Bengal, India
April 1991

Plate 11

29

Plate 12

Under the Curved Tip of the Feather

The most difficult
is not the journey,
but the return—
these days of isolation,
empty streets like set designs.

Reaching out for friends,
I look into their faces and know
they see with closed eyes
because they have not left their country—

while I know only the feeling of my wings,
how the muscles move and stretch
under the curved tip of the feather.

After seven year pilgrimage
Castle Valley, Utah
November 1997

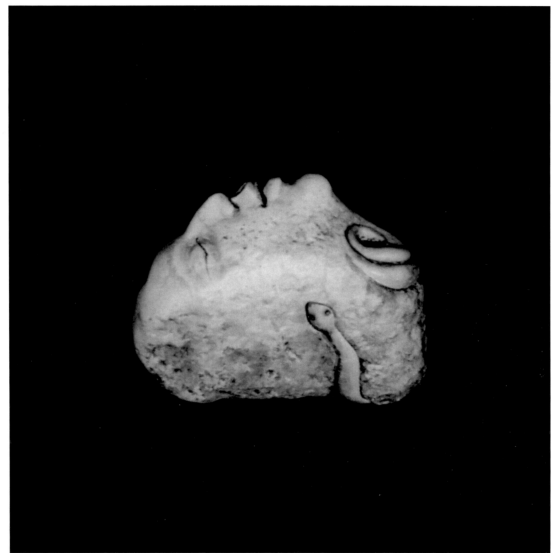

Plate 13

Earth's Kin

Earth speaks as snake,
as sun-baked clay,
as sandstone rising
to rouse the soul
from ancient sleep.

Listening clouds,
am I mineral flesh,
red river blood
and alabaster bone,
reaching—
to find my kin?

Tombstone, Arizona
March 2000

"Ode to a Stone"

Plate 14

Earth Rising to Greet My Love

You come to me in memory even now—
as I write, or walk in rain, or plunge my fingers
into red earth, or press against a sun-baked stone,
or dip my hands in silty waters of the Colorado.

You come to me in memory of your warmth,
as you spread my legs with your thighs,
releasing my hot sulfur springs
that lay body open and soul bare.

We sit in Taos Inn, in shadow.
You hold a glass of coke and rum,
I breath in the music, draw in
rhythms of the drum beat muscle pound.

You reach out and hold my hand—but I feel
anger running through your veins
from past butchering of your race,
soothed for a moment by the rum.

I am still in love with your touch,
earth comes alive and draws your hand
across my breast. But I was the one who said no!
Even now—as you hold another woman,

touch her white skin drunk with pursuit
to find the lips of entry into her soul—
I can feel your warm earth touch, as if she were me—
you drawing power from her kiss and emptying her.

Revenge on the white race
to break and heal all at once
with medicine power in your heart
stitched inseparable from your pain?

Even now, I feel your long black hair
still running cool through the fingers
of my hand, your dark arms
warm around me, drawing close,
earth rising to greet my love.

Taos Pueblo, New Mexico
November 2001

Sweet Silence

For many years I carried sorrow
that I did not have a soul mate.
My friends were finding true life partners.
My own days were without a lover—
in the night I cried out, *where are you?*

One luminous moonlit night I woke
and discovered my Beloved by my side.
In dark leaf mold, I smelled his scent.
On warm night breeze, I felt his touch.
As wolf he wooed me with his song.

He gave me daisies in the spring,
and in the shadow of the mountain valley
stripped me to my Naked Wisdom.
In the lightning crack, he broke my seal
and in the pounding rain, entered me.

Oh, Sweet Silence: nectar of your kiss.

Arcosanti Ranch, Arizona
July 1995

Plate 15

WATER

Rivers of Heart

When Logic Wavers

What stirs in my bone is starlight.
What touches my lips is burnt clay.
What cradles each ankle is sea tide.
When logic wavers another truth sprouts
from the moist warm earth,
rising to greet the day.

Amazon rainforest
August 2002

Plate 16
Following pages: Plate 17

La Selva, the Jungle

La Selva, you sing to me as I climb the stones
that birthed my bone and pulled me out of darkness.

What wild hands gather me now, La Selva,
to hold me in your green embrace?

My roots ache to be tree. My breast rains.
My fingers sprout, infused by your springs.

A rush of cells unfurl their source, pulse
through my thighs, uncoil the vines of my heart.

Seized by humid hunger
entangled as jungle prey,

my soul churns like water into clay,
uncertain, ready to be molded by your dark hands.

Ecuadorian Amazon rainforest
July 2002

Plate 18

A Woman in Egypt

At midnight in a hut by Red Sea,
a respite from my lone travels,
I awaken out of dream, startled
as door is quaking, hinges unscrewed.
    I brace
      the racking door,
      one arm thrust forward,
      scissors clutched in hand,
      eyes bulging
      Kali's breath
      flaming
      in my
      belly.
Open. Open, breathlessly he chants,
Open. Open, he pries the door,
unscrews last hinge.
Tiger rises from my belly,
unearthly roar leaps out:
Le, Le! No, No!

    Kali! Kali! Kali!
    I am a woman
    yes, yes, yes,
    and must walk
    Kali! Kali! Kali!
    freely in this world.

Plate 19

Desert of Egypt by the Red Sea
1990

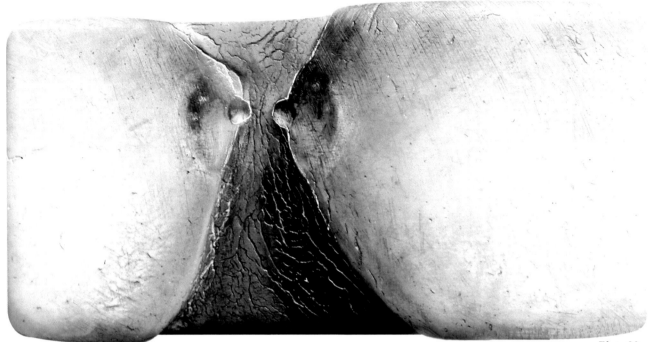

Plate 20

It is the Women Who Heal

It is the soft women's bodies
touching with care,
the soft white down feathers,
the dark breasts of ravens
that love each other,
saying it is all right to be vulnerable,
to be afraid,
with soft bodies,
with hands touching wounded places,
fingers on soft bellies.

It is the women
who heal each other,
who heal themselves,
who show men
how to heal.

Boney Mountain, California
1986

Plate 21

Plate 22

Strong Women of Yelapa

We meet on the jungle path
or by the granite sculpture
as my hammer and chisel
chip away the hours.
These are women grown strong
who found healing
from the wounds
of violence,
physical scars across the face,
internal scars closing
the doors of life.
We are ripe now
tending our souls
with tools of our art
in Yelapa, Mexico,
a garden without walls.

We recognize each other.
Few words said.
Our bodies know,
and relax—
deep in the layers
of memory,
with that glance
of recognition.

Stepping in the river
we splash and laugh
with delight and sadness.

Yelapa, Mexico
Fall 1982

This Woman Woven of Dark and Light

Woman of the dark,
temptress,
murder reddening her hands,
fingerprints of death.
Her night shroud
of voices hushed
are lies of words unsaid,
deception in her trail of wooing,
poison milk the innocent suck.
Her cunt draws men into their death.
Woman of the dark.

Woman of the light,
love weaves the friendship,
and with a lightning strike
dispels the darkness of illusion,
cracks the binding shell of fear and rage.
She lines her bed with radiant life,
nourishes with milk compassion.
With her hair she dries their feet.
Her burst of song fills the soul,
beneath her hand, men are drawn
into the light.

Woven of dark and light, this woman
dances with a demon strength,
lioness is her beauty and her gait,
growling and scratching the earth,
she protects her cubs, all children of earth,
tames with wholeness in her leap,
turns poison into healing love,
dances dark with the light of life,
calming war to the stillness of peace,
and with her single eye,
gives clear sight—
this woman of dark and light.

Santa Barbara
California 1973

Facing Page: Plate 23

Plate 24

Plate 25

Deep Ocean

The deep
　　ocean of spirit
　　　　sets me in motion,
　　　　moves me as the winds blow,
　　　as the storms move across the sky,
　　as the moon pulls tides
　tumbling me
over stones and sand,
trembling with joy.

Inspired by the song of the mid-19th century
Netsilik Eskimo Shamaness, Uvavnuk
Castle Valley, Utah
January 2004

51

Amazon Jungle

I walk for the first time
into the heart of the Amazon,
shaking off the city
with each step.
Green jungle vines
fold just-born tips
over dying stalks.
Swollen cloud bellies
thunder rain,
clearing hot moist stillness
with cool patterned beat.
Swelling camellia-rivers
change sky blue to silver.
Shipibo Indians bathe nude
along the banks
and smile, a child's smile
in a grown-up's face.
Grandmother folds aging arms
around new born babe.

I stand on the red path weeping
as frayed strands of L.A. fall away.
I long to hold life here in hand,
to weave vine, stalk, mud and babies—
a basket to carry back to my homeland.

Puculpa, Peru
1977

Facing Page: Plate 26

FIRE

Fire Under Stone

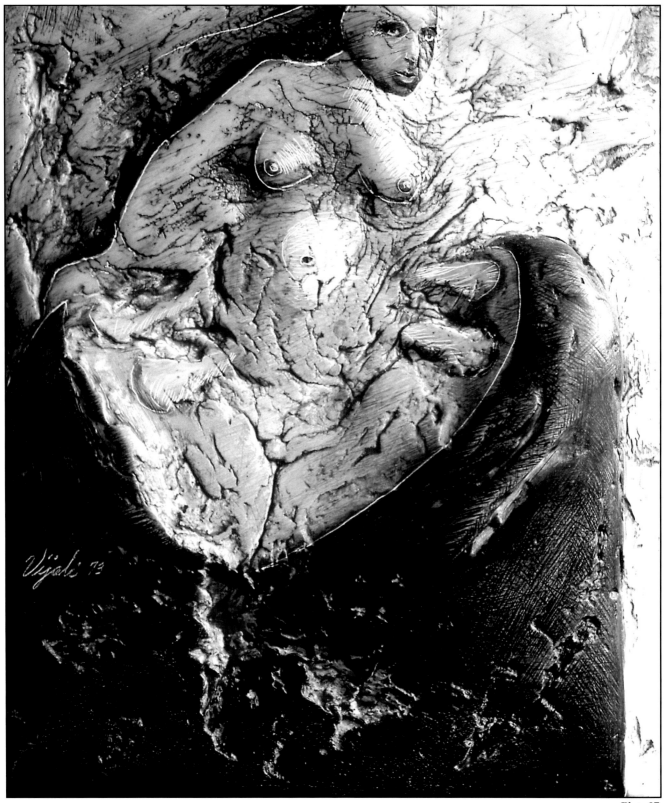

Plate 27

Fire Poem

My sadness
is not so much from red tongues
licking at the sky-light well,
or willows gathered by my hand
for my sacred space where I live alone.

My sadness
is not from the crackling timbers
that were cut and gathered
from the mountains at La Sal,
stripped of bark to pale smooth flesh,
nor the billowing black smoke
vomiting her undigested meal
across white polished walls
that were curved so fine
as hand turned pottery.

My sadness
is not from the burnt hay bale walls,
nor the melted sky-dome,
nor the death of books
signed by friends with love notes
that turned to ash.

My sadness
is because you,
who might have had tea with me,
would not be walking in
my front door sited to greet the rising sun.

You, who might have kissed my lips,
become my lover, would not be there—
friend, unknown lover—you.

Castle Valley, Utah
November 2000

Black Kali

Smell of the fire's excrement
clings to my hair, my hands, my clothes,
Black Kali, Dark Kali, Night Kali.

In one hand holding a sword of destruction
wildly last night you danced in my home.
With fingers of flame you made a black shrine,
igniting white walls, incinerating rafters,
firing mattress, sheets and pillows,
vomiting fogs of smoke and soot,
scorching my eyes as you lay
a black blanket over windows and floors.
Black Kali, Dark Kali, Night Kali.

In the other hand you gave me peace—
these whisperings in early morning:
"Reminder, reminder, reminder:
You—larger than body,
home—larger than house.
The *world* is your family and home."
Black Kali, Light Kali, Day Kali.

Castle Valley, Utah
November 2000

Plate 28

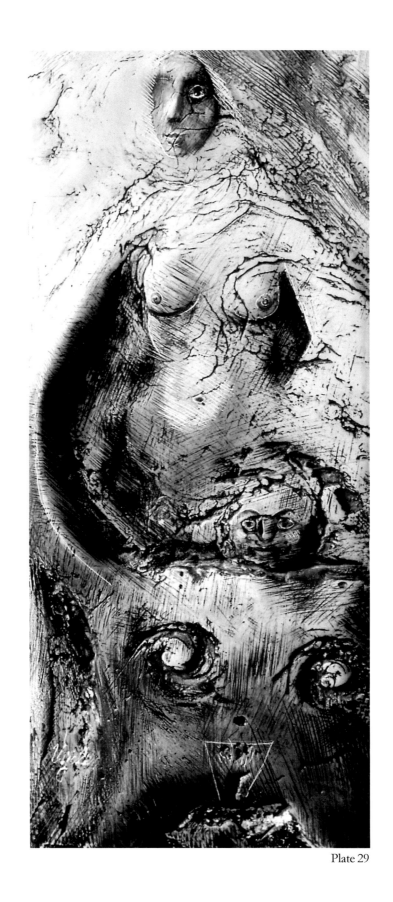

Plate 29

Compost of Love

"Look in my eyes,"
you said years ago,
holding my hand.
But that moment of fire
is almost forgotten.

Where does love go
and where does it end?

Holding your letters,
I read and read—
but now in death
where are you,
full flesh under skin,
man who loved me?

How does love
bite into bone?
My thighs open
to hot days,
steaming rain,
and other loves.

Are they all now
the fingers of ripening soul
as I write these poems,
as I carve these stones—
or lips of the swollen dawn
when I wake with the rising sun
joyful to start my day?

Are you now
a compost of love
from layers of time—
giving richness to days
as turning of leaf mold
enriches the earth?

Upon reading P.'s letters
Arcosanti Ranch, Arizona
Hot summer 1994

The Place a Buddha Sits

As I shiver in the night
in my sleeping bag,
I think of you
sitting in my heart,
the place a Buddha sits,
on soft pink lotuses with stems
that grow within my belly.
I am thinking of you,
dark skin, delicious almond eyes,
soft hands groping,
heart pressed against my heart.
We part—a wail rises from my soul.
My wish is not for time to stop,
I know we'll never see each other—
but for us, for whom a soft touch
was our only lovemaking—
to not be separate
in the boiling of my heart.

Himalayas
India 1999

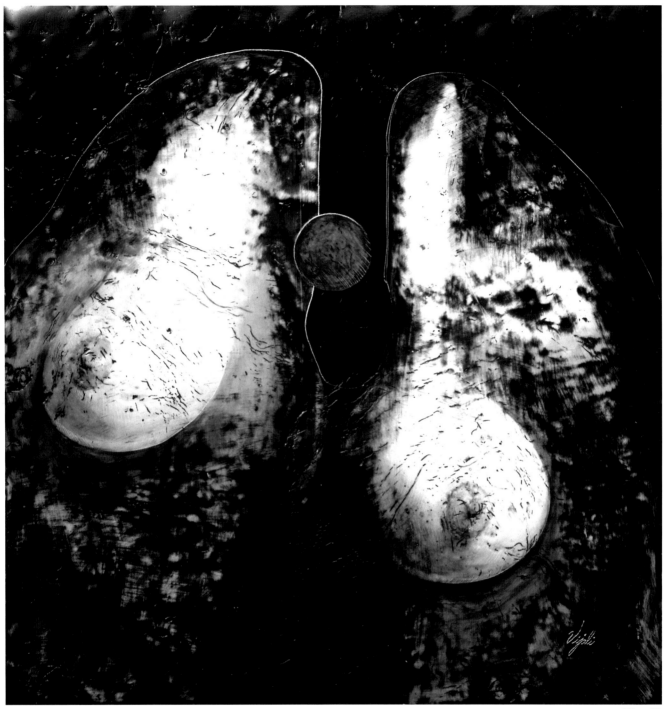

Plate 30

She Walks in Darkness

She walks in darkness
through the ponderosa pines,
as memory pounds within her heart.
And with the rising moon,
she finds her rocky trail
that draws her home.
Just as she left it, blue lamp
stands by bed, red book on the table.
But she has changed.
She does not want to read,
but longs to kiss his lips again.

With morning light
she pulls the curtains closed
to lie in bed, to dream
his hand upon her breast again,
as blood flows hot into her thighs
and breaks up the darkness in her flesh.
His touch brought forth a buried memory
of lovers with their blood so dense with life
that flowers, deer, the breasts of women rise.

Plate 31

Topanga Canyon, California
August 1998

Plate 32

Dark Roots Luminous

I sank in a red stone bowl of darkness,
the cave that held me like a mother's womb,
thinking I was alone, cut off from life.
My dark roots held me buried deep,
not knowing I would ever see the light.

Snake skin shed as old stuff cast off to wind,
this flesh rose out of earth and stone.
A fire burned within, a torch of life
"Hold off this corridor of light," I said,
"so blinding, I do not know where I am."

Now knowing I was not alone. Stitched
in folds of my darkened gown was family.
As I rose, I touched their fingertips and toes.
As I walked into the street, flanking limbs
and thighs, I felt my feet, my dark roots luminous.

Castle Valley, Utah
September 2003

67

Plate 33

Fire Under Stone

With first light,
my feet pulled by all I love
pressing on dry desert ground,
I reach the stream.

Mud-cloaked earth
is cracking in the sun.
On warm sandstone
I sit beside the golden weeds.
Shedding original secrets,
grass gathers in luminous wheels,
earth stands up dancing.

How can I share this moment?
My voice is
fire under stone
sealed by Gods.

Ranch at Arcosanti, Arizona
June 1994

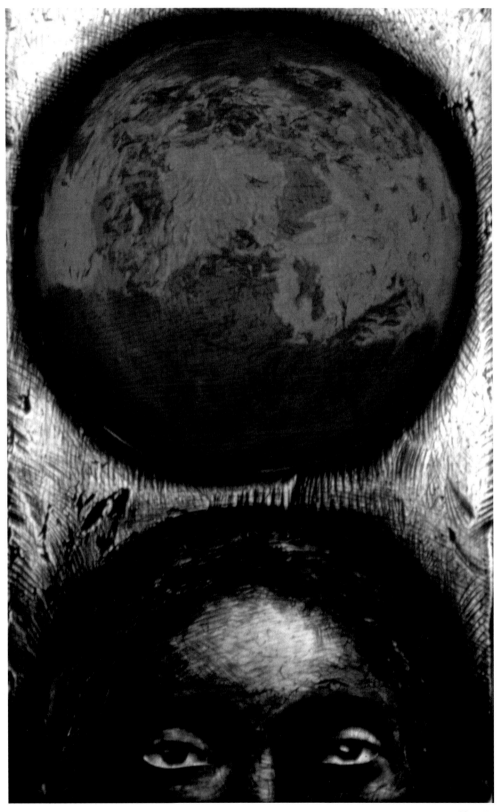

Plate 34

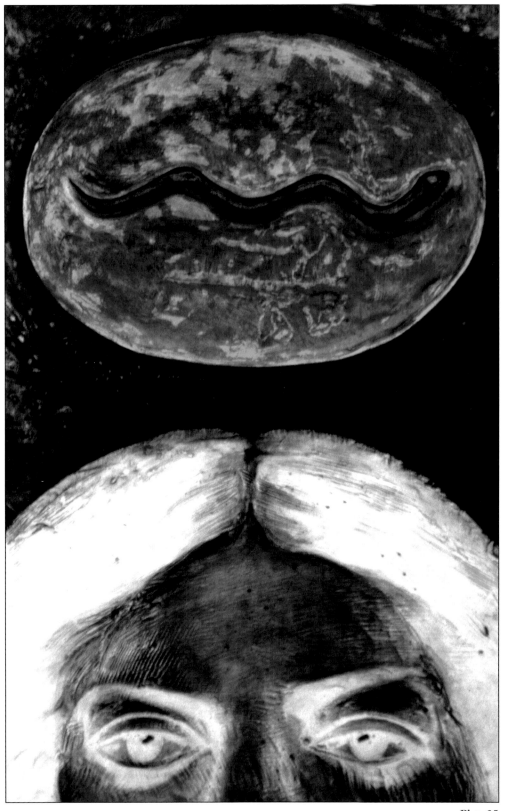

Plate 35

We Wait for the Season of Ripening

Come
to the forest
of life.

As we enter
the darkness
to find
the light,
sun,
shining
through trees,
giver of fire,
flame of life,
enter our bodies,
the divine house.
We wait
in the dark
for the season
of ripening.

Castle Valley, Utah
March 1999

Plate 36

Wine from My Own Heart

How can I
say prayers with words
given through the minds of others,
when my own lips are trembling with song,
a wine from my own heart with the wild taste
of earth that makes my feet dance upon
the warm and sun-baked clay,
under the deep and
darkening sky.

Boney Mountain, California
December 1983

In the Fields of Life

In the fields of life
I have made
myself strong
as a lion,
beautiful
of face.
With gifts
I have come
before you
to walk
among
the living
in the company
of flames,
with my name
upon the water,
my mouth
to the earth
rejoicing.

Desert of Egypt
Fall 1990

Plate 37

74

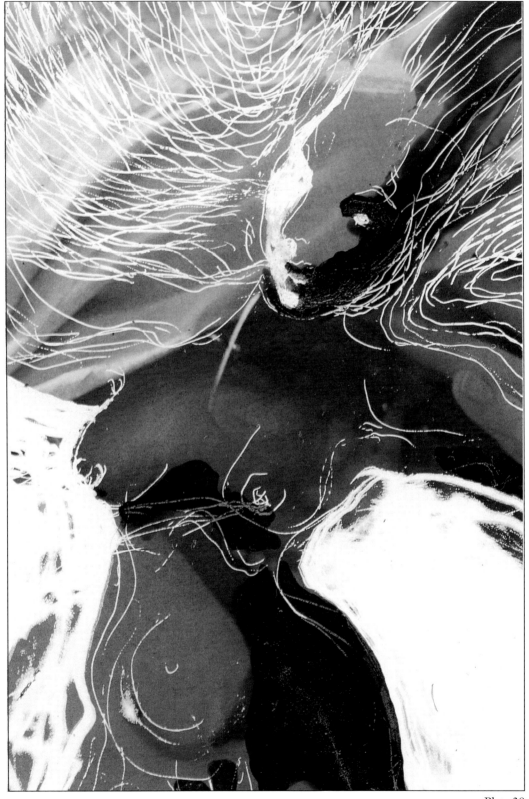

Plate 38

AIR

A Dry Leaf Falls

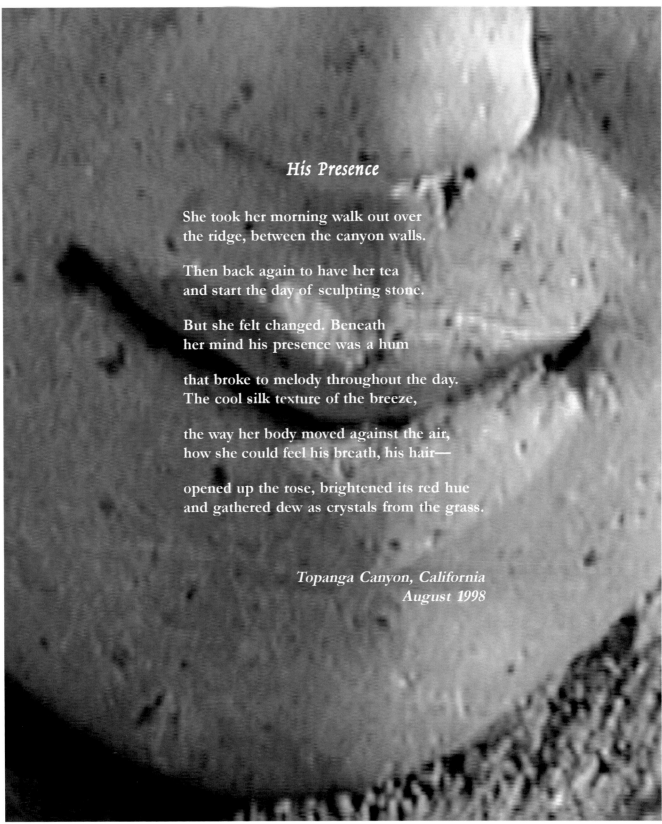

His Presence

She took her morning walk out over
the ridge, between the canyon walls.

Then back again to have her tea
and start the day of sculpting stone.

But she felt changed. Beneath
her mind his presence was a hum

that broke to melody throughout the day.
The cool silk texture of the breeze,

the way her body moved against the air,
how she could feel his breath, his hair—

opened up the rose, brightened its red hue
and gathered dew as crystals from the grass.

Topanga Canyon, California
August 1998

Plate 39

78

Listen

(sing with nature sounds)

Listen   (bag of stones)
listen to beat of stones
tumbling down stream.

Listen   (breath)
listen to howling wind
tearing through trees.

Listen   (drum)
listen to wings of birds
flapping in rhythm
on their migration.

Listen   (two black stones)
listen to lightning crack
connecting earth and sky.

Listen   (cymbals)
Listen to thunder
rumbling on in our bones.

Listen   (rain stick)
listen to roar of water
cutting our canyons.

It is our voice forgotten,
heart beat of the earth our body.
It is our song, the music
of all living things.

Arcosanti Ranch,
Arizona 1993

The Other's Shade

I lay my sleeping bag
by the great stone wall
sculpted by storm and ice,
painted with lichen,
orange, black, and green.

As the night sky
drifts over the desert,
the twisted arms
of the old juniper tree
circle round me,
sheltering me
from dust and wind
as the juniper itself
is sheltered
by this wall of stone.

We need each other
in this fierce desert world,
growing strong
within each other's shade.

Castle Valley, Utah
Vision Quest, October 1997

Death of a Juniper Tree

Seven hundred years the juniper grew
through winds fierce as a sword's cutting edge,
through icy winter and falling snow.

Murdered in a moment
by a neighbor's chain saw.
A hasty choice
and the deed is done.

No prayer can bring it back
to its twisting beauty and centuries
of turning desert green fingers
toward the furrowing sun.

Castle Valley, Utah
March 1997

Plate 40   81

A Dry Leaf Falls

Autumn. Walking red earth path
that runs beneath the maple tree,
a dry leaf swirls when caught by wind.
Reaching out to catch the speckled dancer
my own hand looks about the same
with spots and specks and fine blue veins.

Fall. With turn of colors,
red and yellow, gold and brown…
the thinning of the stem
a burst of flame ignited
before winter's ballet.
My own life is filled with
painting, sculpting, dancing.

Winter. Coming.
What choreography lies ahead?

EarthWays House
Malibu, California
1991-1999

Plate 41

Plate 42

Song to Sky Jewel Man

Dedicated to the Nagpas of Tibet

Forever I have been
a bird flying in the sky
singing my song alone
tumbling downstream as stone,
sitting as a mountain.

But now I have seen a man
of sky and bone, made like me—
birdsong, sandstone, and mountain.

I love you Sky Jewel Man
knowing you are
walking on this earth,
wild haired man of sky mind
now smiling as the radiant sun,
now breathing as the dancing wind,
now sitting as a mountain.

Inspired by meeting
Lama Pema Samdup and Lama Tarchin
Shoto Terdrum, Tibet
Spring, 1992

Plate 43

Joy on Her Lips

Early morning dream
is woven into dawn.
Still warm
under down covers
one arm reaches out
into the cool air,
caressed by soft presence
of all that is loved:
shadow of the mountain,
scent of piñon pine.
She watches
through the window,
green fingers opening
in the warming air,
waiting for the touch of sun.
She too only slowly opens,
fingers reaching
to touch the day, smiling,
joy on her lips.

Castle Valley, Utah
October 1997

Plate 44

Plate 45

Delicious Silence

Delicious silence
   filled
      with sun-drenched leaves
        pushed
          by earth's
           warm
             breeze.

Santa Monica Mountains, California,
Fall 1982

Stillness

Stillness comes whispering,
the first breath of mesa breeze
into the grave of day—
is stone in its silence, receiving the moment,
layered sunset, moonlight, star.

Stillness comes when the corners of mind rest
and the gray squirrel lounges in the setting sun
after gathering seeds for the winter,
when the mule deer stands locked in mutual gaze
and we know each other's tongue.

Stillness comes when sorrow
knits the heart gaping
and the blood stained hands tremble
gathering bones to make an altar,
and winds from the canyons taste of sacrament.

Stillness comes slinking when a gray fox,
timid at first, finds her home
in the strewed rusty cans left by miners,
in the mound of uranium tailings
seeping into the Colorado River.

Stillness comes when the body
lies cool in the moist ground,
and autumn blows amber over the jagged earth,
and the first snow dusts her crystals
on the blood red stone.

Castle Valley, Utah
Election Day
November 2, 2004

Plate 46

ETHER

Soluble

Plate 47

Vision Quest

I lie upon the ground as moon rises
painting silver light across an old stone wall.
My face is marked with sadness as I sleep.
As I'm embraced by rock, a cold wind whines.
The sharpness of night pierces my sleep.

I dream. Wolves set me on fire.
Eagles swoop down singing,
and gather my ashes. We sail
over the desert, then alight.
My ashen feet press against
blood soaked earth.

The sun is rising over red plateaus
warming the air. I look at my hands,
my feet, the red earth beneath me—
What wolf spirit can transform my life?
What eagle song can lift me with its cadence,
breathe space into my too-tight life,
breathe spirit into the harsh edge of my days?

I wait, wait, as the moving winds gather,
circling overhead.

Castle Valley, Utah
Vision Quest, October 1997

93

Plate 48

Nameless One

Nameless One,
I only know how to make love
moving against form:
trees and stones and mountains.
The hardness of your shape enters me
as I encircle the flesh of your form.

Nameless One,
your vastness I cannot grasp
or hold in my mind.
Come closer, will you!
Take shape again
so I can touch you with my hands,
feel you press hard into my form,
bite, hold fast.

Amazon Jungle Peru
Fall 1977

Shattering

I said,
I shall meet You
face to face. Now,
I am humbled calling
out your name pleading
for protection in this shattering
vastness of Your face.

Puculpa, Peru
1977

Plate 49

Kali

Oh mother,
every drop of water
holds your name.
Are you not the light
I see at my forehead
as I fall asleep
slipping into the flesh
of your darkness?

Arcosanti, Arizona
Fall 1994

Night

The unknown tugs upon my nights
and loosens my tied wings and teases
dreams from lips and plays
with strands of tangled hair.

I lie content to dream,
at home in darkness, dense starlight,
and drift as wings come set me free
as I lose hold of stone, and bed...

and take me up, these unknown
wings of space I've grown in the dark,
when stillness lights upon the valley bustle
and I settle in my silent soul...

and take me up and out, and up
a pleasant ease as if the rains of day
evaporate, no duty rises now
except to let my spirit free.

My finger tips are pulsing,
changed to angel wings
transformed by falling night
and silence, the passageway.

Let me die, yes let me die
this moment so complete
and not be changed again from angel
by the business of day.

Plate 50

Night at Castle Valley
December 1998

98

Plate 51

Night Sky Draws Me Home

As I lie on my cot
beneath piñon pines,
night sky draws me home.

Day breaks over red plateaus
as Christ is born again and again.
Bobcat, eagle, juniper tree
come bearing gifts
throughout the day.

Night comes again,
I return to my cot.
Cathedral black sky with billions of lights
pulls me home.

Castle Valley, Utah
1997

Plate 52

Plate 53

Not Who You Think I Am

My friends say I am artist
circling the globe.
But I know: *I am stone.*
My scent is sun baked rock.
I slowly change with wind and rain,
standing watch in utter calmness,
not twitching a finger,
lichen on skin, orange, chartreuse, green.

My friends believe I am a sculptor
chiseling rock.
But I know: *I am water*, ever moving.
Concealed by jacket and skirt,
I flow inside but no one sees.
My seaweed hair is tied.
Patiently, over and over and over,
I bite into shore sculpting earth,
as earth molds my form.

My friends see I am five foot one.
But I know: *I am air,*
ever present breath
carrying scent of sage
or decaying flesh alike.
Giver of life
and when I withdraw,
giver of death.

My friends whisper, "She's calm as a nun."
But I know: *I am fire,*
always kindled.
I know the heat
with which I burn,
crackling as I change lives,
my dancing tongue licking,
red mouth devouring,
hopes for the future
turn to ash.
Fire alone causes my movements.

I've no other motive
than rising as phoenix.

My friends hear I am fifty-five.
But I know: *limitless space am I.*
I weep when I gaze into sky.
Black night is my original mind,
my eyes, stars defined.
And yet I steer the wheel
driving on L.A. freeways
#405 South
making my 2 p.m. appointment,
space moving into space,
I am unlimited.
From the steering wheel,
my fingers reach out
past edges of the universe.

EarthWays House
Malibu, California
July 1993

Touch

Red bedrock beneath my hand,
blue breath upon my lips—
the opening in earth
from which we came.

I stumble over valleys,
over ruins of ancestors,
over rivers cutting canyons,
over your limbs outstretched.

And here I find the essence
of all that flies, and walks, and swims,
laid buried waiting to touch my hand.

Castle Valley, Utah
May 2006

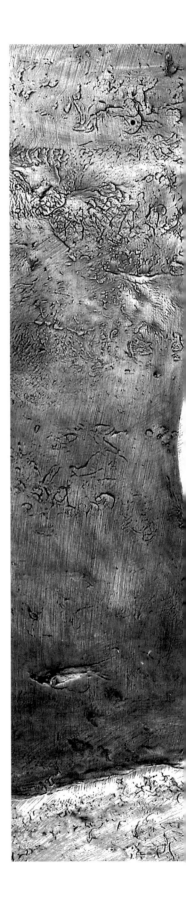

Plate 54

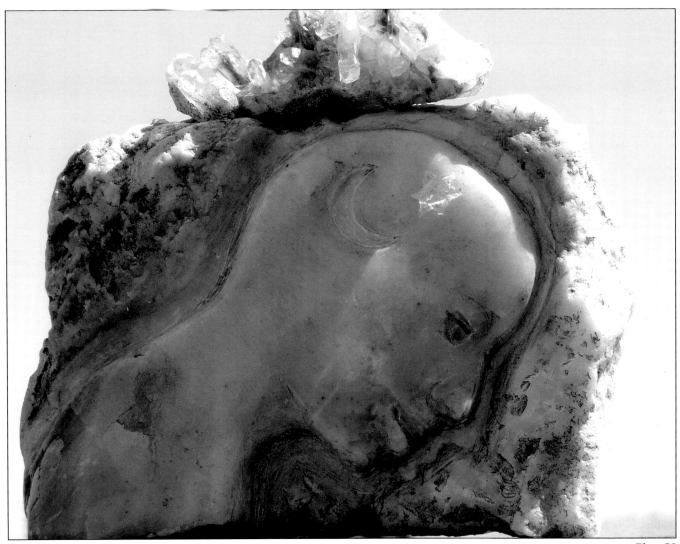

Plate 55

Sky Woman

Vast sky
radiant sun
steady mountain
deep sea
am I.

Can you
love me as I am:
uncontainable,
earth, sky
woman?

Castle Valley, Utah
June 2005

Beneath a Banyan Tree

In a tiny Bengali village
I sit beneath a Banyan tree
and my heart is won...

A child brings garlands
lays them round my neck.
She dances, eyes blazing
skirts whirling yellow and blue.

The full moon rises crisp
as Mara brings spiced tea.
Her husband Basu Dev
with closed eyes begins to sing:

At source we're all the same.
We are fruits of the Tree of Life.

Now, can you tell me, friend,
what difference is there
Hindu or Muslim,
Man or Woman? Blood is red,
each heart beats rhythm of life.

Inspired by the Baul song
"Shoblo Ke Koi"
Shambati village
West Bengal, India
1991

Of Water & Fire & Stone

From wind and water,
from mineral baths
beating on stone, I came.
From moss and pine,
agate and sapphire
tumbling in flame, I came.
From fusion of cells,
dividing and parting,
dying in flesh, I came.

On the waters always, I was.
Spirit rising from stone, I am.
In the earth and wind, I remain.

Castle Valley, Utah
September 2003

Plate 56

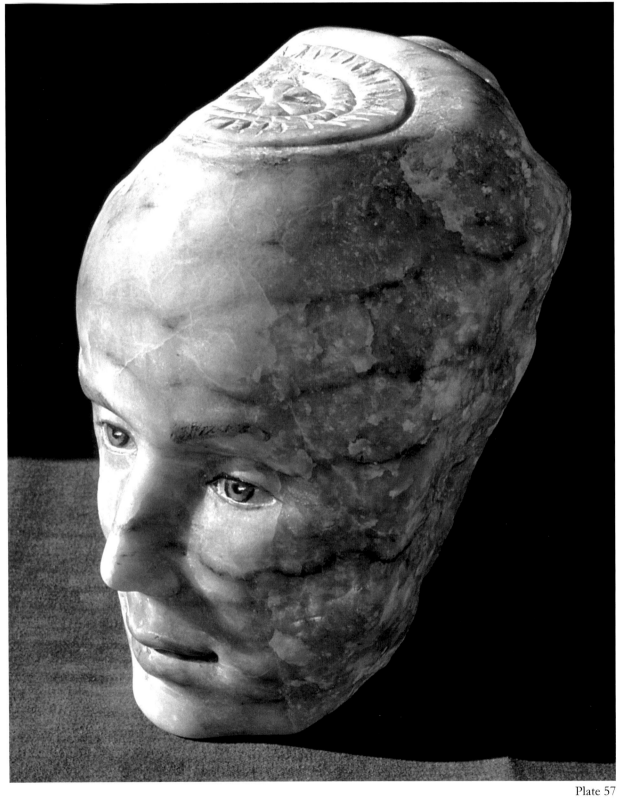

Plate 57

Soluble

Dark earth path
is shadowed by cloud.
Pensive, I walk
a serpentine trail
to the slate blue lake.
Dark swing of mind
is a flick of God's eyelash
in the bright glaze of water.
The still surface reflects
the snow capped range
of the La Sal Mountains.
One gust of wind ripples the face,
and mountains disappear
to black depths of water.

Oh, are we that still moment
between breezes
made soluble
in an instant?

Castle Valley, Utah
March 1998

Artwork by Vijali Hamilton

EARTH—Blood Red

WATER—Rivers of Heart

FIRE—Fire Under Stone

AIR—A Dry Leaf Falls

ETHER—Soluble

Vijali Hamilton is a visionary multimedia artist, sculptor, poet, musician, perfromance artist, and author. Over one thousand of her artworks are in museums, public places, and private collections. Early in her life she spent ten years as a monastic member of the Vedanta Society convent. Later she received her Masters in Fine Arts from Goddard College and has lived as a working artist since. In 1986 Vijali founded the *World Wheel: Global Peace Through the Arts* Project, a seven year pilgrimage during which she circled the globe creating monumental stone sculptures and established *Theater of the Earth* in twelve countries lying close to the 34th north parallel. She has since begun a second *World Wheel* which will circle the equator beginning in the Andes and Amazon of Ecuador. The *World Wheel* Project endeavors to bring understanding within and between communities, countries, and individuals as a means to further peace on our planet.

Vijali has published two books of poetry and artwork: *In the Fields of Life,* and *Liberty Enlightening the World,* and also one book of non-fiction and artwork: *World Wheel, One Woman's Quest for Peace.* With Edie Hartshorne she has composed a CD of music: *Awaken Your Heart From Its Ancient Sleep,* and created a film: *World Wheel, One Woman's Pilgrimage for Global Peace.* Her art, writing, and life have been presented in a number of books, articles, radio interviews, and television documentaries, including: *Cultural Creatives* by Paul Ray and Sherry R. Anderson; *Goddess: A Celebration of Art & Literature,* edited by Jalaja Bonheim; and *Mandala, Journey to the Center* by Bailey Cunningham.

Sri Kali Yantra, ancient east Indian symbol for the divine feminine, womb of the cosmos, carved by Vijali.

Acknowledgments

Thank you Jay Salter, friend and poet, with gratitude for your help in editing these poems, to Peter Levitt, Shirley Graham, Cris Coffey, Laura Kamala, Andrew Beath, Patricia Hopkins, Henry Swan III, and Peter Marin for your editing eye, to Edie Hartshorne and Monette Tangren Clark for your creative input, to Henry Swan III, Markell Brooks, and Dale Clark for your support in making this book possible. Thank you Terry Tempest Williams who has always believed in me and my work. Thank you Chick Hebert for rescuing me from technical disasters, to Karen Fisher and Sara Glaser for helping me with the book design, and to Henry Swan III for your guidance and image editing. Thank you Dale Clark and Steven Smith for your photography, and thank you Dale for your encouragement and enthusiasm during the '70s when a good many of these images were created.